Learn to Play
MAH JONGG

Learn to Play
MAH JONGG

MARCIA HAMMER

David McKay Company, Inc.

NEW YORK

Library of Congress Cataloging in Publication Data

Hammer, Marcia.
Learn to play mah jongg.
1. Mah jong.   I/ Title.
GV1299.M3H17   795'.3   78-32026
ISBN 0-679-14375-0

3 4 5 6 7 8 9 10

Manufactured in the United States of America

With appreciation to my Husband, Warren, who taught me to believe "as a Man thinketh, so is He"; and to my Daughters, Melodie and Debbie, whose excitement drove me onward. This book is dedicated to the three of them, and the Friday night crew.

Contents

Introduction

Here is the chop suey of table games. It sounds Chinese, it looks Chinese (and indeed once was Chinese), but it has been considerably Westernized—that's MAH JONGG! It is an old Chinese gambling game which at one time was played only by men. Until the last century, Mah Jongg was confined to the yamen of nobles, but it has now been seized upon by cultured people all over the world. Today in China, men and women alike play, although it is now frowned upon by the Chinese Government. They favor a more physical activity for their people, yet Mah Jongg continues to flourish. As part of their New Year's celebration, the Chinese still play Mah Jongg for three days and three nights *continuously*. Mah Jongg is a big gambling game in Chinatown, New York, where $500 to $3,000 can be lost during one session.

After thirty centuries, Mah Jongg has emerged from the walled palaces of princes and mandarins, and it is the most engaging indoor game that has ever come to American shores. It is felt that the game had its origin in the 12th Century B.C. and probably developed from dominoes. It is believed that Mah Jongg was first played as early as the time of Confucius, and it was imported to the United States in 1920. The game incorporated the rules from both North and South China, where the playing differed somewhat, before it was introduced to this country.

The name "Mah Jongg," which means "the sparrows," was coined and registered by Joseph P. Babcock, a United States resident of Shanghai. He introduced the game to this country, modified the rules and gave the "tiles" English titles. The tiles are small rectangular pieces, at one time made exclusively of ivory. Today, however, they are made of bone, bamboo and plastic as well. I have even seen a wooden set made primarily for children. The complete set ranges in price anywhere from $10 to thousands of dollars, based on the quality. A prominent New York City shop features just the Mah Jongg tiles for $1,500, but the least expensive set is as effective as the most costly. It is virtually indestructible and will last more than a lifetime.

The tiles were originally engraved with symbols used in the Chinese Army. They were once called "spears," "targets" and "vans." The spears were the weapons, the targets were the objects aimed at, and the vans were the rewards. When the game was taken over by civilians, the spears became bamboos, the targets became circles, and the vans became characters. The names of the symbols were further changed, and today they are called "Bams," "Dots" and "Craks," respectively. Sets sold in the West usually have Arabic numerals in one corner of a suit tile, and letters denoting the four Wind tiles. The One Bam (or bamboo) tile depicts a symbolic bird. Chinese tiles have similar characters, but the numerals and letters are omitted.

Before World War I, each Chinese province had its own style of play and dialect name for Mah Jongg. In an effort to standardize the game in this country, the National Mah Jongg League was formed in 1937, with headquarters at 250 West 57th Street, New York, N.Y. 10019. The National League publishes an instruction booklet and a yearly-revised standard-hand card. Today, Mah Jongg is a fad throughout the United States, England and Australia, although it is played virtually everywhere in the world. One can go to Bulgaria, Canada, Central America, Dominican Republic, Finland, Germany, Holland, Hong

Kong, Indonesia, Israel, Italy, Japan, Korea, Mexico, Puerto Rico, Republic of Panama, South Africa and Sweden, and find Mah Jongg enthusiasts.

Women by the thousands are leaving their daily chores, neglecting their families and spending hours every day playing the ancient game. There is even a chance that the Mah Jongg parlors of Hong Kong may someday replace the OTB parlors of today. More and more men in this country are playing Mah Jongg, and couples find that it makes an enjoyable social evening. Tom Seaver, the sensational National League pitcher, plays Mah Jongg; Jackie Gleason and Art Carney learned the game a few years ago; Bruce Lee, of Kung Fu fame, was a Mah Jongg enthusiast; and Dwight D. Eisenhower and Winston Churchill played at one time.

Though the simple rudiments of the game are readily mastered, the finesse with which it can be played comes with the experience of the player. Mah Jongg is both a game of skill and chance. The same hand recurs infrequently, which adds to the interest and fascination. Mah Jongg is identical in principle to rummy. After mastering the nomenclature, a good rummy player usually has no trouble with Mah Jongg.

Learn to Play
MAH JONGG

I

Bim–Bam–Boom

*"To know what you know, and know what you don't know,
is the characteristic of one who knows."*

—*Confucius*

Mah Jongg is a table game played by a minimum of two and a maximum of six players, five being the most preferred and most enjoyable. The complete set consists of the tiles, racks, dice, chips and better, which all fit compactly into a carrying case. (See Figure 1.)

Mah Jongg is similar to the game of rummy in that both games require the players to form "hands," the actual formation of which will be explained in the chapter "Intelligent Interpretations."

As of this writing, the complete Mah Jongg set contains 152 tiles. This figure may vary from one year to another when there is an addition or deletion of Jokers and/or Flowers. In Chapter III, you will learn when this change takes place and

Fig. 1

what to do about it. For now, it is important to learn to identify the tiles. The construction of American sets makes it much easier than it seems. The simplest way of memorizing the tiles is by breaking them down into groups.

SUITS

There are three suits represented:

Dots — Each tile in this suit has a number in the upper left-hand corner. There are the same amount of circles on a Dot tile as the corresponding number. In the Dot suit, the numbers run from 1 to 9. There are four of each of these tiles. Outlined below is the Dot suit and the name by which each tile is called.

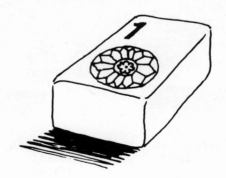

Fig. 2
One Dot

Fig. 3
Two Dot

Fig. 4
Three Dot

Fig. 5
Four Dot

Fig. 6
Five Dot

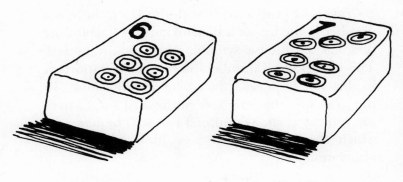

Fig. 7
Six Dot

Fig. 8
Seven Dot

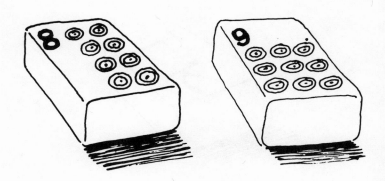

Fig. 9
Eight Dot

Fig. 10
Nine Dot

Craks — In this suit, as with the Dots, there is a number in the upper left-hand corner. Each of the tiles has a Chinese symbol, which is always red. The inclusion of numbers is especially important in this suit because it facilitates identification. In the Crak suit, the numbers run from 1 to 9. There are four of each, as outlined below. The name by which the tile is called is written beneath the illustration.

Fig. 11
One Crak

Fig. 12
Two Crak

Fig. 13
Three Crak

Fig. 14
Four Crak

Fig. 15
Five Crak

Fig. 16
Six Crak

Fig. 17
Seven Crak

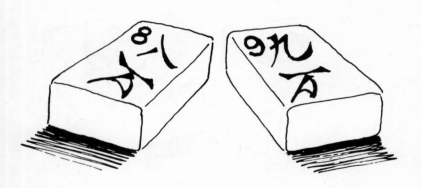

Fig. 18
Eight Crak

Fig. 19
Nine Crak

Bams — There is a number at the top of each tile in the Bam suit with the exception of the Eight Bam, which has its number in the center of the tile. The symbols on these tiles are bamboo twigs, the same number of twigs corresponding to the number on the tile. The markings are generally green, with an occasional red marking on the 5, 7 and 9. The color, however, has no bearing on the tile. The One Bam is somewhat different from the rest of the Bam suit in that it is illustrated by a symbolic bird. The One Bam differs slightly from one set to another, and for this reason it is advisable to have this tile identified for you when playing with an unfamiliar set. Three One Bams from three different sets may be seen in Figure 52, found in the next chapter, "Blossoming Beginnings." The Bams run from 1 to 9, and there are four of each tile. Below is an illustration of each, with the name by which it is called.

Fig. 20
One Bam

Fig. 21
Two Bam

Fig. 22
Three Bam

Fig. 23
Four Bam

Fig. 24
Five Bam

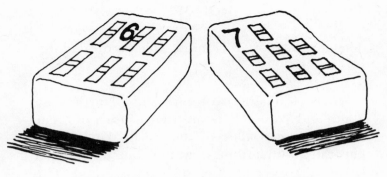

Fig. 25
Six Bam

Fig. 26
Seven Bam

Fig. 27
Eight Bam

Fig. 28
Nine Bam

11

HONORS

The next category is Honors, which is divided into two groups:

Winds — There are four Winds: North, East, South and West. There are four of each of them, making sixteen tiles in all. Each Wind tile is illustrated with a Chinese symbol, but in the upper left-hand corner an English letter is found. This simplifies reading the tile—"N" appears on the North tile, "E" is on the East tile, "S" is for South and "W" stands for West. So you see, what appears to be typically Oriental is really a camouflage for an Americanized version of Mah Jongg. Below are the four Winds.

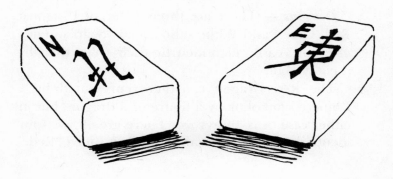

Fig. 29
North

Fig. 30
East

Fig. 31
South

Fig. 32
West

Dragons — There are three different Dragons: Red, Green and White (also called "Soap"). They are more easily identified by their color than by their symbol.

The Red Dragon is either represented by a Chinese symbol or by a figure of a dragon, but in either case, it is always *red*. There are always four identical Red Dragons, and this tile is called "Red."

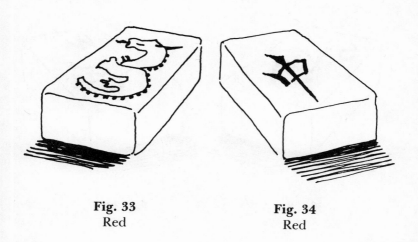

Fig. 33
Red

Fig. 34
Red

The Green Dragon is illustrated by a Chinese symbol or dragon, always *green* in color. This tile is called "Green," and there are four identical Greens in a Mah Jongg set.

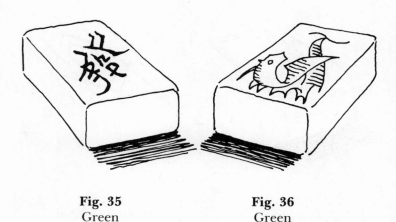

Fig. 35
Green

Fig. 36
Green

The White Dragon, depending upon the particular set in use, will be a completely blank tile (sometimes edged in blue), it may have a dragon outlined in blue, or it may be represented by a geometric-like figure. This tile is called "White" or "Soap." There are four identical Soaps in a set.

Fig. 37
White (or Soap)

Fig. 38
White (or Soap)

FLOWERS

Flower tiles are not illustrated identically in all sets. However, they differ so greatly in appearance from the aforementioned tiles you should have no difficulty in identifying them. The design on these

Fig. 39
Flower

tiles depicts some type of flower. Some Mah Jongg sets have numbered Flowers, but this has no bearing on the game. As of this printing, eight Flowers are required to complete the set. Although most sets are equipped with extra Flowers, be sure when purchasing a new set that there are several additional ones. If your set lacks the required number of Flowers (or any tile, for that matter), contact the National Mah Jongg League, Inc., at 250 West 57th Street, New York, N.Y. 10019. They can often supply you with the missing tiles which will match your set. Illustrated are three different Flowers, and that is the name by which they are called.

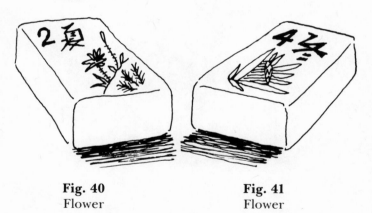

Fig. 40
Flower

Fig. 41
Flower

JOKERS

"Joker" and "Big Joker" are one and the same. As of this printing, eight Jokers are required for the Mah Jongg set. Not all sets are equipped with a sufficient number of Jokers, and many old sets have none at all. To remedy this, extra Flowers can be covered with Joker decals, which can be purchased wherever the Mah Jongg card is sold (stationery stores, particularly). The decals can also be gotten from the National Mah Jongg League. Extra Flowers can also be converted into the needed Jokers by covering them with a piece of colored tape. Below is an illustration of a Joker.

Fig. 42
Joker

Review this chapter until you can identify all the tiles. By doing this, the remaining instructions will be more easily understood.

19

II

Blossoming Beginnings

"When you do not know, not to try to appear as if you did, that's knowing."

—*Confucius*

Before play begins, all 152 tiles are placed face down and are shuffled. Four racks are used, and one is placed in front of each of the four players. (See Figure 43.)

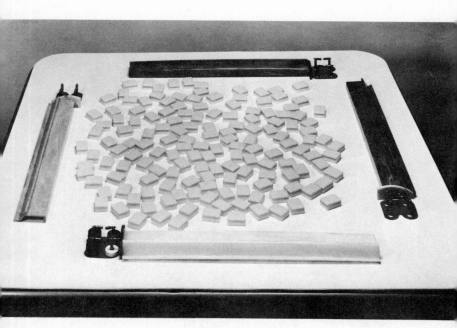

Fig. 43

The following instructions are for a four-handed game. The chapter "Viable Variations" will explain how Mah Jongg can be played with only two or three people. The chapter "Bettors and Betters" will discuss a five-handed game.

THE WALL

Each player places nineteen tiles face down against a rack, then another layer of nineteen on top of that, also face down. These tiles are gathered indiscriminately by the four players, who do the piling all at the same time. The resulting pile is called the "Wall." There are four Walls, one in front of each player. Each Wall contains nineteen separate stacks, and each stack is comprised of two tiles. (See Figure 44.)

Fig. 44

BREAKING THE WALL

Player No. 1, who is called "East," is the one who initiates the play. Each player has a turn at becoming East, and it is generally the host (or hostess) who is the first East. (See Figure 45.)

East
(the first player)

Player #4
(This player
will be East
for game #4.)

Player #2
(This player
will be East
for game #2.)

Player #3
(This player
will be East
for game #3.)

Fig. 45

East begins by pushing his/her rack with the nineteen stacks of tiles to the center of the table. East then rolls a pair of dice and "Breaks" the Wall at the given number. Breaking the Wall is done by:

—first, totalling the two die just rolled
and
—second, counting the stacks as the total indicates, from right to left of East's Wall
then
—holding back the number of stacks (as shown by the dice) against East's rack, and putting them into their original position as when the Wall was first built.

For instance, if a 5 appears on the dice (a total of 3 and 2 or 4 and 1), *five stacks* are counted from right to left of East's Wall. These five stacks are pulled back against East's rack and remain there until the end of the game. They are the last tiles to be used. (See Figure 46.)

Fig. 46

The balance of East's Wall—in this case, fourteen stacks—are the tiles to be picked by the players.

PICKING THE TILES

At this stage, the players will be picking tiles starting with East's Wall.

ROUND 1. East (Player No. 1) picks tiles first, and takes the first *two stacks* from the balance of the Wall which remains in the center of the table. (See Figure 47.)

Fig. 47

Player No. 2 picks the next two stacks of tiles, Player No. 3 picks the following two stacks, and Player No. 4 takes the next two stacks, each picking in turn. Remember that each stack constitutes two tiles. Therefore, each time a player takes *two* stacks, *four* tiles are actually being taken.

As the tiles are picked from East's Wall, eventually this Wall will become depleted (with the exception of the tiles which will remain there until the end of the game as a result of East Breaking the Wall). The tiles will then be picked from the Wall in front of Player No. 4 (the Wall to the left of East). The Wall which is now in play is "curtseyed" to the center of the table. This term simply means that the next Wall to be used is "pushed" away from the rack to facilitate its use.

ROUND 2. East begins the second round of picking. The tiles are taken, two stacks at a time, first by East and followed by players No. 2, No. 3 and No. 4, each player taking the *next* available stacks in turn.

As the picking of tiles continues, the Wall in front of Player No. 4 will become depleted. When this occurs, the next Wall to be curtseyed and used will be that of Player No. 3.

ROUND 3. The third round of picking is the same as rounds 1 and 2.

ROUND 4. East begins the fourth and final round of picking by taking the *first* and *third top tiles*. (See Figure 48.)

28

Fig. 48

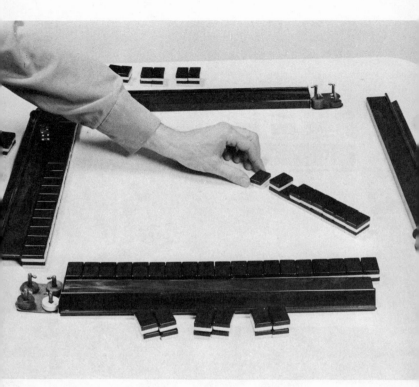

Fig. 49

Player No. 2 takes the first *bottom tile*, which is left exposed after East's pick. (See Figure 49.)

Player No. 3 takes the next *top tile.* (See Figure 50.)

Fig. 50

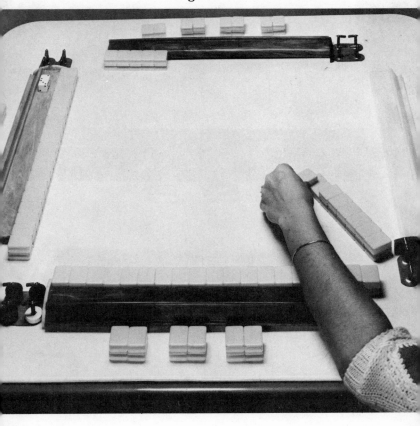

Fig. 51

Player No. 4 takes the next *bottom tile*. (See Figure 51.)

Players No. 2, No. 3 and No. 4 should now have thirteen tiles each, and East should have fourteen tiles. If this is *not* the case, retrace the steps taken, beginning with Round 1.

Remember: The Walls are always curtseyed and used in clockwise fashion (East's Wall first, Player No. 4's Wall next, then that of No. 3, and No. 2's Wall last). However, the players *pick* their tiles *counterclockwise* (East picks first, No. 2 picks second, No. 3 picks third, No. 4 picks last).

At the completion of the four rounds of picking, each player puts his/her own set of tiles on the "ledge" in front of the rack, facing him/her. Each player is now able to view only his/her own complete set of tiles. (See Figure 52.)

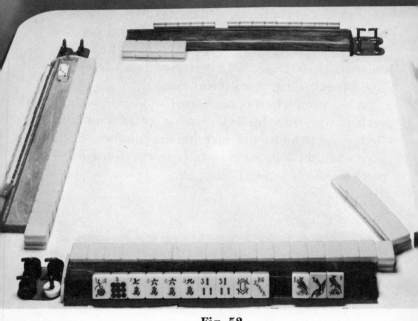

Fig. 52

FORMULATING A HAND

At this point, each player is interested in developing a potential hand. The easiest way to see some semblance of one is by placing the suits together—Bams with Bams, Craks with Craks, Winds with Winds, etc. (See the way the initial thirteen tiles [East has fourteen] are assembled in Figure 52.) The next step is to evaluate which tiles are more prevalent—odds, evens, Winds, singles, pairs, Flowers . . . ? We will delve more deeply into actual hands in the chapter "Intelligent Interpretations." With the original thirteen tiles, it is generally not easy to find a hand; but with practice and experience, you will get the knack of picking out at least one hand to try to assemble.

Tiles alien to the hand you are attempting to formulate will be discarded. Before you are able to determine which tiles should be retained and which discarded, a knowledge of the card, symbols and terminology are imperative. Therefore, the next step is . . .

III

Intelligent Interpretations

"Learning without thought is labor lost; thought without learning is perilous."

—*Confucius*

Prior to 1937, Mah Jongg hands were completely devised by the individual player. As long as fourteen tiles were utilized, the combinations could be whatever the player wanted them to be—three of a kind, four of a kind, a run (1,2,3,4), etc. With the establishment of the National Mah Jongg League, the game has become standardized. A Mah Jongg card was developed, and in whatever state Mah Jongg was played, the same card prevailed. Therefore, it is vital for the card to be fully understood in order to play the game properly.

The National Mah Jongg card is printed each year outlining approximately fifty basic hands. Many of the hands are the same as those from the previous year's card, but every year some of the old hands are deleted and are replaced with new ones. The same card is used for twelve months, from March to March, at which time a new card is in print. The National Mah Jongg League card may be obtained by writing the National Mah Jongg League at 250 West 57th Street, New York, N.Y. 10019.

At the top of the card, a few words are written about the required number of Flowers and Jokers. At the present time, eight Jokers and eight Flowers are needed to complete the Mah Jongg set. However, these figures may occasionally change from one year to another. To be sure the set being used is complete, always check these instructions on the card. A new set provides for these fluctuations by supplying extra Flowers. If the Mah Jongg set has more than the required number of Flowers, remove them. Put the extras away for safe-keeping. They can be used in later years when additional Flowers are needed. When more Jokers are needed, a Flower tile can be covered with a decal that says "Big Joker." The decals can be bought inexpensively from the National Mah Jongg League, or you can have a homemade covering by using a snip of mystic tape.

It is important to know at a glance what the symbols on the card mean.

Intelligent Interpretations

SYMBOL	MEANING
F	Flower
D	Dragon
N	North
E	East
W	West
S	South
C	Concealed (hand)
X	Exposed (hand)

Following the "C" or "X," you will see a number. This is the monetary value of the hand indicated.

The terms found on the card which need defining are:

1. Pung—Three identical tiles.*
2. Kong—Four identical tiles.*
3. Quint—Four identical tiles plus a Joker.*
4. Face Tile—Any tile, excluding the Joker.

*Jokers are the same as "wild cards." They can be used in a hand to replace any face tile—*unless*—a Jokerless hand is being played (as specified on the card). Therefore, "identical" tiles can be all face tiles or a combination of face tiles and Jokers. In the case of a Quint, there must be at least one Joker since there are only four of each tile in the Mah Jongg set. (Five Flowers do not constitute a Quint.)

The card lists hands under different categories:

N E W S	Referring to the Winds— North, East, West and South.
THE YEAR	There are always a number of hands involving the year that particular card is in effect (1978, 1979, etc.).
DRAGONS	Red, White (or Soap), Green.
CONSECUTIVES	A run of numbers (1, 2, 3 or 5, 6, 7 or 7, 8, 9, etc.).
1-3-5-7-9	Where hands utilizing odd numbers are found.
2-4-6-8	Even numbers are used here.
3-6-9	These particular numbers are used.
JOKERLESS HANDS	No Jokers can be used for these hands.
ADDITION HANDS	Occasionally found on the card. This type of hand goes in and out of existence from year to year.
MULTIPLICATION HANDS	Used some years, other years not (same as Addition hands).

Although the hands are listed categorically, at times Dragons may be intermingled with numbers, Winds intermingled with Dragons, etc. In other words, just because a hand is listed under one particular category, it doesn't mean that it can't overlap another category.

When you have picked up the original thirteen tiles, place them on your rack in some order—Bams with Bams, Dots with Dots, Craks with Craks. Put the Winds together as well as Dragons with Dragons; have the Flowers next to one another; group the Jokers. If there are any pairs, Pungs or Kongs, put them together. The above placement will make it easier to see what is more prevalent—a particular suit, the Winds, Flowers, or . . . ?

Try to learn the card; know where to find the type of hand best suited for your distribution of tiles. If you are holding several Winds, check the hands listed under the NEWS category. You may have a combination of even numbers and Dragons, so you would then look under two categories—2-4-6-8 and Dragons, checking to see if this assortment could be utilized together. The more you play, the more you will find the card being committed to memory, enabling you to spot several possibilities at one time.

The card is printed in three colors—red, blue and green, each color representing another suit. When a hand is illustrated in blue and green, it

41

means that hand must be played in two different suits. It doesn't matter *which* two suits as long as they are two *different* ones. Each suit has a corresponding Dragon:

SUIT	MATCHING DRAGON
Dots	White (or Soap)
Bams	Green
Craks	Red

If a hand is illustrated in one color and numbers and Dragons are needed, the suit and Dragons must *match* (as above). If the numbers are one color and the Dragons another, the suit and Dragons must *be dissimilar*.

Printed after some hands is a sentence in parentheses. This tells you if the hand can be played in another way. If there are no instructions in parentheses, the hand must be played exactly as it is illustrated. For example, under the category 2-4-6-8, the last hand on the 1978–79 Mah Jongg card reads:

FFF2222FFF8888

There are no variations to this hand. It must be played exactly as you see it—a total of six Flowers, with four 2's and four 8's of the same suit. You may either play the 2's and 8's in Bams, Dots or Craks, as long as the 2's and 8's are *all Bams* or *all Dots* or *all Craks*.

Under the category 3-6-9, the first hand reads:

$$33366999 \quad \cancel{DDD} \quad DDD$$
$$\text{(blue)} \qquad \text{(red)} \quad \text{(green)}$$

The instructions in parentheses read: "Pung Dragons Other 2 Suits." This means that if the 3's, 6's and 9's are Bams, for instance, there must be three Soaps and three Reds. If the numbers are Craks, the Dragons must be Soaps and Greens. If the 3's, 6's and 9's are played in the Dot suit, the Dragons must be Reds and Greens.

If, during the course of playing a hand, the tiles you pick start to produce another type of hand, you are at liberty to switch from one hand to another.

IV

The Challenging Charleston

"A man can put energy into the process, not the process into the man."

—*Confucius*

No, this is not a dance from the flapper era; it is simply a "passing situation." The Charleston is one way of eliminating unnecessary tiles from your rack with the expectation of receiving strategic ones from those passed to you.

To simplify matters, let us assume that after carefully studying the tiles on your rack against the card in front of you, you have decided to attempt one of the even hands. Therefore, the only tiles you will be interested in securing and saving will be 2's, 4's, 6's and 8's. You will want to eliminate all others that wouldn't conform to the hand you have in mind (Winds, odds, etc.). The following passes are compulsory and are made by all four players.

45

FIRST RIGHT (FIRST PASS)

This is the first compulsory pass, which is made by all players. Begin by removing three tiles from your rack which do not seem to belong. Pass these unwanted tiles face down to the player on your *right*. Your three opponents will also be following this same procedure. You will make your First Right as soon as you've decided which three tiles you will discard (just as the other players will make their First Right when they are ready). All passes are made en masse. (See Figure 53.)

East passes to No. 2.

No. 2 passes to No. 3.

No. 3 passes to No. 4.

No. 4 passes to East.

After you have made your First Right, only then are you permitted to accept the three discarded tiles from the player on your left, which was his/her First Right. In other words, you are not allowed to look at the three tiles passed to you until you pass three of your tiles. (The *compulsory* passes of the Charleston are always made with *three* tiles.) If one or more of the tiles received can be advantageous to the hand you are attempting to play (in this case, it would be any even number),

East

Player #4

Player #2

Player #3

Fig. 53

place the tile (or tiles) you wish to retain on your rack. After receiving your First Right, you may decide not to keep any of the three tiles just passed to you. It is at your option to pass them along as your next compulsory pass, or to interchange them with tiles already on your rack, and give three other tiles as your next pass. You may keep one, two or all three tiles which you received. Retain those tiles which are needed for your hand. While you are making these decisions, the other three players are doing likewise with the tiles they received.

ACROSS (SECOND PASS)

The next compulsory pass is the Across. Again, an evaluation is made, and another three unwanted tiles are selected. This time, they are passed to the player sitting *opposite*. (See Figure 54.)

East passes to No. 3.

No. 2 passes to No. 4.

No. 3 passes to East.

No. 4 passes to No. 2.

As a result of all players making an Across pass, everyone will *receive* three tiles only after they have *passed* three. The same as with the First Right, one, two or three tiles may be kept. If they are alien to the hand, these tiles may be used as the next pass.

As with all passes, you are trying to better your hand. Check your tiles against your card carefully and keep those tiles which go with the hand you are attempting to complete.

East

Player #4

Player #2

Player #3

Fig. 54

FIRST LEFT (THIRD PASS)

The third pass you will make is called the First Left, and is directed to the player on your *left*. (See Figure 55.)

East passes to No. 4.

No. 2 passes to East.

No. 3 passes to No. 2.

No. 4 passes to No. 3.

After the first two passes, you may have developed a "pat" hand (a completed hand). If such is the case, you would not want to make further passes because you would then be giving away the tiles you need. On the First Left, you do not have to pass any of *your* tiles. If you find that you cannot give up any tiles from your rack, you will make a "blind" pass. This is done by taking the tiles passed to you and automatically handing them to the one on your left. This blind pass would then become *your* First Left. You may look at the tiles you are passing blind, but whether you want them or not, once you have made the decision to pass blind, *they must be passed*. Anyone who chooses to do so may make a blind pass on the First Left. If, by chance, all four players developed a pat hand after the first

51

East

Player #4

Player #2

Player #3

Fig. 55

two passes, there would be no First Left. This is a rare situation, and almost never occurs.

You may decide to pass only one tile from your rack for your First Left, thus obligating you to "steal" *two* tiles from the three which were passed to you. In other words, three tiles are passed on the First Left, and they may come:

—entirely from your own rack
—passed blindly (as above)
                    or
—as a combination of tiles from your rack
    and those which you may steal.

If you are stealing one or two tiles, the selection must be made while the tiles are face down. You may look at them *after* they are stolen; however, once the decision to steal has been made, you *must* pass them. Stealing or making a blind pass on the First Left may be made by any one or all of the four players.

After the First Left is completed, each player has the option of stopping the Charleston before its usual conclusion. If even one player decides not to continue, the Charleston ends right there. The decision to terminate the Charleston would be made by the player whose hand is intact and who does not have three tiles to pass. If the Charleston does end after the first three passes, the next step is . . .

OPTIONAL

The Optional is always the last pass of the Charleston. It follows the First Left if the Charleston is prematurely terminated, or it concludes the series of passes if the Charleston is completed. As its name implies, this pass is made at the player's option. One, two, three or no tiles may be passed to the one sitting across from you. (See Figure 56.)

East *may* pass to No. 3 (or not at all).

No. 2 *may* pass to No. 4 (or not at all).

No. 3 *may* pass to East (or not at all).

No. 4 *may* pass to No. 2 (or not at all).

The Optional pass is made after you have asked the one sitting opposite, "How many tiles would you like?" There are no turns taken; all players ask the question simultaneously or separately.

If the answer to your question is "Two," but you prefer three tiles, the exchange must be two tiles. If the answer you receive is "Two," but you want one tile, only one tile will be exchanged. To simplify, the player wanting the *least* number of tiles is in command. If you don't want any tiles

East

Player #4

Player #2

Player #3

Fig. 56

from the one sitting opposite, there is no Optional for you or for your opposite opponent.

PLEASE NOTE: The novice will not stop the Charleston if he/she has three tiles to pass. There are times when an experienced player will stop the passing even if he/she has three unwanted tiles to pass. This will be discussed in the chapter "Timely Tips."

If the Charleston is *not* stopped after the first three passes, only then do the following passes take place.

SECOND LEFT

This pass becomes compulsory if the Charleston is not stopped after the First Left. All players must pass three tiles on the Second Left—no stealing or blind passes are permitted here. The pass is made to the one on your left—three tiles, face down. (See Figure 57.)

East passes to No. 4.

No. 2 passes to East.

No. 3 passes to No. 2.

No. 4 passes to No. 3.

East

Player #4

Player #2

Player #3

Fig. 57

ACROSS

The Across is compulsory, made up of three tiles, passed face down to the one sitting opposite. The tiles you pass on the Across must be selected from the thirteen you are holding (East, however, is holding fourteen tiles). Again, there is no stealing or blind passing for this pass. (See Figure 58.)

East passes to No. 3.

No. 2 passes to No. 4.

No. 3 passes to East.

No. 4 passes to No. 2.

East

Player #4

Player #2

Player #3

Fig. 58

FINAL RIGHT

The last pass you will make to the player on your right is called the Final Right. (See Figure 59.)

> East passes to No. 2.
>
> No. 2 passes to No. 3.
>
> No. 3 passes to No. 4.
>
> No. 4 passes to East.

On the Final Right (the same as with the First Left), a blind pass or a steal may be made. (See "blind" pass and "stealing" under First Left.) No blind passing or stealing is permitted other than on the First Left and Final Right.

East

Player #

Player #2

Player #3

Fig. 59

OPTIONAL

After these last three passes, which are made only if the Charleston has not been stopped after the *first* three passes, there is an Optional pass. It is at the player's discretion to pass one, two, three or no tiles to the one opposite. To repeat an important rule—the player wanting the least number of tiles is in command.

Remember, the Charleston may be stopped *only after the First Left* (which is actually the third pass of the Charleston). If it is not stopped at this time, the Charleston must be carried out until its conclusion.

By the time the Charleston has been completed, you should know exactly which hand you will try to complete. The experienced player will have several possibilities in mind, but for the beginner, one will suffice.

If you memorize the following terms which are used for the Charleston in this exact order, you should have no difficulty with the opening plays of the game.

First Right
Across
First Left
Second Left
Across
Final Right
Optional

If the Charleston is stopped after the First Left, only the following passes would take place:

> First Right
> Across
> First Left
> Optional

V

Ploy of Play

"By nature, men are nearly alike; by practice, they get to be wide apart."

—*Confucius*

Now that the preliminaries and Charleston have been explained, the actual playing of the game takes place. Each player will try to form a completed hand, which is comprised of fourteen tiles. The card must be followed closely in an attempt to simulate one of the hands indicated. If and when this is done to completion, player has Mah Jongg. These are the steps which will lead to Mah Jongg:

As a result of the original pickup of tiles, East has fourteen tiles while the remaining three players each have thirteen.

EAST (First Player)

makes the opening play by discarding one unwanted tile, one which doesn't fit into the hand East is attempting. East announces the name of the

65

tile and places it face up on the table. East now has thirteen tiles.

PLAYER NO. 2 (Player to East's Right)

picks the first available tile from the Wall. In Figure 52, you will see that the first tile to be picked is a *bottom* tile. As a result of this pick, Player No. 2 will have fourteen tiles. If this fourteenth tile is needed by Player No. 2, it is placed on the rack while a tile which doesn't fit into the hand is removed. Player No. 2 "throws" the unwanted tile face up on the table and declares its name. If the picked tile is not needed, Player No. 2 throws it out and calls its name.

PLAYER NO. 3 (Player to the Right of No. 2)

picks the next tile from the Wall, evaluates its need, and throws out one unwanted tile while declaring it.

PLAYER NO. 4 (Player to the Right of No. 3)

picks the next tile from the Wall, decides whether or not it is needed, and throws out a tile which is not needed. The thrown tile is announced by Player No. 4.

If a declared tile is needed by any of the players, it can be gotten under certain conditions. This is explained under the heading "Exposed Hands."

The cycle repeats itself with East, who plays again by picking the next tile after No. 4 has discarded. Remember, the tiles are picked one at a time, in turn, and all discarded tiles are called by

66

name by the player throwing it. The hand is continually changing with each pick. As stated earlier, the object of all the picking and throwing is to ultimately achieve a completed hand as indicated by the card, which is Mah Jongg.

As was mentioned in Chapter III, there are two types of hands—Concealed and Exposed.

EXPOSED HANDS (AS DESIGNATED ON THE CARD)

When a player is attempting to complete an Exposed hand, there are two ways Mah Jongg can be made:

1. The player may pick his/her own tiles, in turn, from the Wall.
2. The Exposed hand may be improved and/or completed by the player "calling" a tile which has been thrown by another player. The term "calling" simply means that a declared tile is taken by the player who needs it. Calling a tile may be done out of turn.

If any one of the players throws a tile which is needed to complete a Pung (three of a kind), Kong (four of a kind) or Quint (five of a kind) in another player's *Exposed* hand, the tile may be called. When a tile is called, the completed Pung (Kong or Quint) must then be exposed on top of the rack of the player who made the call. (See Figure 60, which shows an exposed Kong.) Once an exposure has been made and a discard thrown, the exposure may not be altered in any way.

Fig. 60

A tile may only be called if it *completes* the Pung, Kong or Quint. A tile may never be called if it simply completes a pair. The one exception here (as is also true in a Concealed hand) is that if a declared tile is needed for Mah Jongg, it does not matter if it completes a pair, if it is the only tile of its kind in the hand, or what it actually completes—all that matters is that it is Mah Jongg for the player calling it, and, therefore, it may be called.

CONCEALED HANDS (AS DESIGNATED ON THE CARD)

There is only one way a player can improve a hand when going for a Concealed hand. The player must pick his/her own tiles, in turn, from the Wall. If a declared tile is needed to complete a Kong, Pung or Quint by a player attempting a Concealed hand, that tile is "dead" as far as he/she is concerned. The declared tile cannot be utilized for the Concealed hand. There is, however, one exception to this rule. If a declared tile is needed *for Mah Jongg* and for Mah Jongg only by the player attempting a Concealed hand, that tile may be called for Mah Jongg. To simply *improve* a Concealed hand, no tiles may be called. A player may convert a Concealed hand into an Exposed hand at any time, which would then enable the

69

player to call for exposure (to complete a Pung, Kong or Quint).

An Exposed hand, therefore, is somewhat easier to achieve than a Concealed one, because the player has two ways of getting a needed tile—by picking it from the Wall or by calling it.

When a tile is thrown and declared, it may be needed for exposure by one or more players attempting an Exposed hand. It could also be needed to complete Mah Jongg by a player (or players) attempting an Exposed or Concealed hand. Who gets the tile? The rule is:

1. If more than one player wants the same declared tile for an exposure, the player whose turn would come next is the one to receive that tile. For instance, if East were to throw a tile and players No. 3 and No. 4 both want to call it, Player No. 3 would be the one to receive it because his/her turn comes before No. 4's turn. If Player No. 4 throws a tile which is needed by both East and No. 3, East would be the one to receive the tile because East's turn comes before No. 3's turn.

2. If more than one player wants the same declared tile for Mah Jongg, whether it is the player attempting a Concealed hand

or the one attempting an Exposed hand, the player whose turn would follow the declarer first receives the tile for Mah Jongg.

3. If more than one player wants the same declared tile, one needing the tile for Mah Jongg while the other needing the tile for exposure, the player who needs the tile for Mah Jongg has precedence. It does not matter, in this case, whose turn is next—the player who will make Mah Jongg with the declared tile receives it.

BUT—a player may not call a tile (neither for Mah Jongg nor exposure) if that tile has been "covered." Covering a tile means that the succeeding player has already thrown and declared a tile. In other words, the opportunity to call a tile is lost after the next tile has been thrown.

A *Pung* is complete when you have *three* identical tiles.

A *Kong* is complete when you have all *four* of the same tiles.

A *Quint* is complete when you have *five* of the same tiles.

A Joker may be used to complete any of the above, but a Joker *must* be used for completing a Quint since there are only four identical tiles of each symbol.

71

A Pung is completed in several ways. To facilitate the explanation, let us assume a Pung of Wests is needed. Player may:

1. pick all three Wests. If this is the case, the Pung remains concealed on player's rack (whether or not the hand is a Concealed or an Exposed one).
2. have two Wests in own hand and may then call the third.
3. have one West and one Joker in the hand and may then call the third West. (The Joker may be used as one of the Wests. Remember, a Joker, which is "wild," may be used in place of any tile.)
4. have two Jokers in the hand which could be used as Wests. Player is then entitled to call the West if it should "fall" (if it is declared by one of the players).
5. pick three Jokers, all of which could be used as Wests. Player may not call a tile to complete a Pung unless he/she already has a pair in one form or another (as above).

Whenever a tile is called to complete a Pung, the entire Pung must be exposed on top of player's rack after the call is made.

A Kong, which constitutes four like tiles, may be completed in many different ways:

1. by picking all four tiles yourself (in which case you do not expose it on top of your rack).
2. by having three of the face tiles and calling the fourth.
3. by having two face tiles and using a Joker for the third, enabling you to call the fourth.
4. by having one face tile with two Jokers, enabling you to call the fourth.
5. by having three Jokers, thus being able to call the fourth.
6. by having four Jokers, all of which can be used for the needed Kong.

Whenever a tile is called to complete a Kong, the entire Kong must be exposed after the call is made.

A Quint, which constitutes five like tiles, may be completed in several ways (a Quint of Wests will be the objective here, to simplify the explanation):

1. by picking all four Wests yourself plus a Joker (in which case you do not expose it on top of your rack).
2. by having three Wests and a Joker, then calling the fourth West.
3. by having two Wests and two Jokers, then calling another West.

73

4. by having one West with three Jokers, enabling the West to be called.
5. by having four Jokers, enabling the West to be called.
6. by having five Jokers, all of which can be used as the needed Quint.

When a call is made, the declarer of the tile passes it to the one calling it. The caller now has fourteen tiles and it is, therefore, that player's turn to throw and declare a tile. If East calls a tile, for instance, that tile is passed to East who, after exposing the Pung, Kong or Quint, throws off the fourteenth tile. Player No. 2 follows East by picking and throwing. Whenever a tile is called, the one calling the tile then becomes the next one to throw a tile, and the picking and throwing is resumed by the next one in line. When a call is made, there are times when a player (or players) will miss his/her turn. Unless the called tile is passed directly to the declarer's right, one or two players will miss their turn.

Each player is entitled to call tiles for one or more exposures. Whenever a call is made, an exposure must be made. There will be times when a player will have as many as four exposures on top of rack. If more than one exposure is made, the opposing players will be able to determine the type of hand being played and should then attempt defensive maneuvers, trying not to throw any more tiles toward that hand. There will be times when the experienced player will throw his/her own "safe" tiles in preference to throwing a tile which is known to be needed by another player. This strategy will be discussed in the chapter "Timely Tips."

When an exposure is made after a tile has been called, a Joker (or Jokers) will often be part of the exposure. Let us say that two Wests were exposed with one Joker. The first player to pick another West may replace the Joker with that West. The exchange can only be made when it is the turn of the player who has the West. An exchange may also be made by a player who happens to have the West in his/her rack.

Once a player replaces a Joker with a face tile, the Joker cannot be used to call a previously declared tile. After the Joker is replaced, player can only do one of two things—declare Mah Jongg or throw and declare an unwanted tile. If a player has several Joker replacements, all of the exchanges can be made at once—*but*—only when it is the player's turn.

Play resumes as above until one player has used all of the tiles, the thirteen on the rack (Concealed and/or Exposed) plus the one picked (or called), making fourteen tiles in all, to form a completed hand. When this occurs, the player has Mah Jongg. Each Mah Jongg hand has fourteen tiles. The fourteenth tile may be a picked tile from the Wall or a called tile which another player has thrown and declared. A player may call a declared tile for Mah Jongg whether or not the hand is Concealed or Exposed. Remember, the only time a call can be made for a Concealed hand is for Mah Jongg.

It is extremely rare, yet possible, for East to have Mah Jongg at the end of the Charleston. Since East is the only player who initially has fourteen tiles, this is the only player who could conceivably make Mah Jongg as a result of the interchange during the Charleston. This is so unusual that you could play a lifetime and never see it happen.

When a player has Mah Jongg, the game ends. If all four Walls are depleted, there are no tiles left to be picked and no one has made Mah Jongg, it is a "Wall" game. In each game there is only one winner—either a player makes Mah Jongg or the Wall wins. An average game takes from five to fifteen minutes, depending on how quickly someone makes Mah Jongg.

VI

Money Matters

"Men do not stumble over mountains, but over molehills."
—Confucius

Playing for some incentive, no matter how small, seems to add another dimension to the game. It is fun to play for money, and somehow, when you do, it becomes a better game. The players try harder and the play in general is different than when no stakes are set up.

On the Mah Jongg card, there is a price given for each completed hand. The least expensive is 20¢, which would be the easiest hand; the next is a 25¢ hand; then 30¢; and 35¢, which is the most difficult to make. The actual amount paid to the winner will vary, depending upon the amount that will be wagered in total. In most games, the price indicated on the card is the figure used.

The player to make Mah Jongg with his/her *picked* tile receives double the value of the hand. If the tile is *called* for Mah Jongg, the player who threw the Mah Jongg tile pays double while the other players pay the single price. In a game where there are bettors, the bettor pays or collects in the same manner as the one on whom bet. (The subject of betting will be thoroughly discussed in the following chapter.)

When there is a bettor involved, the players will, at times, be paying as much as *four times* the actual value of the hand. To explain: If East made Mah Jongg with a *picked* tile, East would collect double the value of the hand. If East was bet on, the remaining three players would have to pay East *and* the bettor double the value.

In most Mah Jongg games, a limit is placed on the amount one can lose. The set amount is called "Pie." There are some games where the Pie is as little as $2 while others are as much as $20, with different set amounts for Pie in between these two figures. There is an occasional game here and there where there is no limit.

A Pie game is a more sociable type game and less of a gambling one. The beginner should certainly not play in a game where there is no Pie. If a game has a $5 Pie, the player who has exhausted that amount continues to play the game but is no longer obligated to pay any more winners until he/ she has recouped some of the losses. The bankrupt player is "on Pie" and will collect from the other players if he/she makes Mah Jongg, but no longer continues to pay another winner. If a player who is on Pie wins a hand and then has money once again, this player does not pay back any of the losses which were incurred during the time Pie. However, once the player has regained some money (it does not matter how much), the obligation to pay future winners is reinstated.

When a player is on Pie, he/she can collect if Mah Jongg is made, but will not pay if another player has Mah Jongg. It often happens that a player who has been Pie throughout most of the games ends up a winner, simply because he/she won the last several games. Some may feel this is not fair, but it is a good way of keeping the losses to a minimum. Actually, if you continue to play with the same people, you will find that everyone will be in this position from time to time, and what is fair to one becomes fair to all.

With each Mah Jongg set there are five racks, each containing different colored chips. There is a hole through the center of each chip, enabling it to be housed on the pegs found at the left end of each rack. Each color represents a different monetary value, which will vary depending upon the stakes of the game. Each player must start with the same amount of "money" and pays the winner of each game from his/her stack. The "money" you collect for winning is placed on your own rack.

At the end of a session, each player counts his/her chips. The chips in excess of the original stack will total the amount won; the chips missing from the original stack will total the amount lost. The players pay or collect as their individual stacks will indicate. If the amount won does not balance that which has been lost, a mistake was made in the counting of the chips.

Although many games continue to use the chips, the figuring and confusion which arise can be eliminated simply by using money at the onset. If you are playing a $5 Pie game, each player should put that amount into some kind of container, being careful not to confuse one container with another. When someone makes Mah Jongg, the losers take the amount to be paid from their individual containers. Likewise, the money won is placed in the winner's container. At the end of a session, there is no need for figuring. The money won or lost can be determined at a glance.

There are some, but few, unlimited games. I do not advise the novice to play in an unlimited game for obvious reasons.

When playing in a game where the Pie is very little ($2 or $3), an adjustment of the prices listed on the card should be made. Otherwise, if one player lost three consecutive games, you would immediately have a player on Pie. The balance would be off if someone lost all their funds that quickly. To prevent this from happening, a hand marked 20¢ on the card could become a 5¢ hand; a 25¢ hand could become 10¢; a 30¢ hand, 15¢;

and a 35¢ hand could then be 20¢. By doing this,
the money would last longer. The players would
not go Pie quickly, and the winners would be able
to collect from the losers for a longer period of
time. It is more fun for a winner to be able to
collect from all players, no matter how small the
amount.

If, after the last tile is picked, no one has made
Mah Jongg, it is a "Wall" game—no player has
won, but the Wall has. A Wall game marks the end
of the game, and no one pays or collects unless the
bettor has bet on a Wall game. If this is the case,
the bettor receives a predetermined amount from
each player. The usual amount is 25¢ per player,
but this figure may vary from one game to another. The price for a Wall game is always established before the game has begun.

When there has been a Wall game, some groups
will collect a predetermined amount from each
player and bettor, which is put into a "kitty." The
kitty continues to build up as there are more Wall
games. The first player to complete a Jokerless
hand collects the kitty, in addition to being paid by
each player. The kitty can be saved from session to
session until a Jokerless hand is made, or the kitty
can be distributed among all players at the termination of a session when no Jokerless hand has
been made. Although this is not in the rules of the
game, having a kitty adds another dimension. If
the kitty becomes sizeable, more Jokerless hands

will be attempted. This will result in more Wall games, since Jokerless hands are so difficult to achieve.

A kitty could be established to compensate a winner when one or more players have gone Pie. A set amount can be collected from the winner of each game and/or from each player after Wall games. The kitty would pay a winner the amount that could not be collected from the Pie player or players.

Another kitty which can be formulated is used for a "bonus." Each player donates $1 before the session begins. A timer is set for approximately thirty minutes. The next player to make Mah Jongg after the timer rings collects a dollar from the kitty in addition to being paid by the losers. If the winning hand was bet, the dollar is split between winner and bettor(s). The timer is set for as many times as there are dollars in the kitty.

Establishing a kitty is optional and should be decided upon by all participating.

VII

Bettors and Betters

"The cautious seldom err."

—*Confucius*

In a game where there are five or six players, four will sit and play while the other one or two will be onlookers. They will not be part of the game until it is their turn to sit and play. To add more interest to the game, especially for the outsiders, they should be allowed to make a bet.

At the termination of the Charleston, each bettor walks around the table and looks at each of the four hands. There is no discussion between player and bettor, nor between the bettors. In a game where there are two bettors, each of them writes his/her bet on separate pieces of paper. After both bettors have made their bet, they may discuss it with one another; but the bets are not to be disclosed to the players until after the game is over. If they discuss their bets with the players or reveal their bets before the end of the game, the bets are cancelled.

In a game where only one person bets, the bet is made on a better. (See Figure 61.)

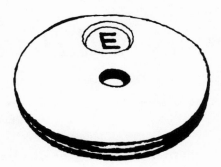

Fig. 61
Better
(showing East was bet on)

The better is a round double disc which, when turned, will reveal an "E" (for East), a "2," "3" or "4." These four denominations represent the four players seated at the table. The better is turned to the number which represents the player the bettor thinks will win that game. (Figure 61 illustrates how the better looks when East is bet on.)

When the bet has been made, the better is turned face down and is not to be touched until the end of the game. At the termination of the game, the better is upturned to reveal the bet to all players. If the winner was chosen by the bettor, both bettor and winner collect the set amount (as shown on the card) from the remaining players. If the bettor did not bet on the winning hand, the bettor must pay the winner.

The winner of the game receives double the price listed on the card from all players if the Mah Jongg tile was *picked* from the Wall. When the winner *calls* a tile for Mah Jongg, the player to throw that tile pays double the value of the winning hand while the other players pay the single figure. (See the chapter "Money Matters" for amounts to be paid.) If an incorrect bet was made, the bettor pays the same amount as the one on whom bet has to pay. Bettor is entitled to bet on East even if East has Mah Jongg at the end of the Charleston.

If, after viewing the hands of the four seated players, the bettor feels there will be no winner, the dial is turned to the symbol shown in Figure 62.

Fig. 62
Symbol for Wall Game Bet

This is another marking which appears on most betters, which, in Chinese, means "East." However, this symbol is used to indicate that the bettor has made a "Wall bet." The bettor, in this case, does not think anyone will make Mah Jongg. If all the Walls have been depleted and there are no more tiles to be picked, the Wall is said to have won the game. If a Wall bet was made, the bettor collects a predetermined amount from each player (25¢ is a fair amount to establish for Wall bets).

On some betters a "W" will appear in place of the Chinese symbol shown in Figure 62. Dialing to the "W" would also indicate a Wall bet was made.

If the bettor makes a Wall bet but a player wins the game, the bettor is obligated to pay double the value of the hand made.

When the bettor is trying to decide on which hand to bet or whether a Wall bet should be made, many factors should be taken into consideration. First, use the process of elimination. Discard those hands which are furthest from Mah Jongg. If five or more tiles are needed to complete a hand, this would not be a particularly good bet. The following is a good rule of thumb in determining the bet:

1. The hand closest to Mah Jongg is usually the best bet.
2. If more than one player is attempting the same hand, it would generally not be a wise bet to choose either of them.

However, one of these two would still be a consideration if:

a. the hand contained several Jokers.

b. one of these players was on call (ready for Mah Jongg).

c. one of these players was one from set (needing two tiles for Mah Jongg).

3. If more than one player has a good hand, bet on the easier one. For instance,

a. a Call hand (also referred to as an "Exposed hand") would be simpler than a Concealed one.

b. an Exposed hand needing a Kong is easier than one requiring a Quint.

c. a Jokerless hand is the most difficult to complete, especially if it is a Concealed hand and the player is not set for Mah Jongg.

4. You may want to bet on a Jokerless hand because the player is one from set. However, the remaining players are utilizing the needed tiles. This would be a very poor, if not impossible, bet.

5. When there is more than one good hand on which to bet, the ease of the hands and the number of needed tiles being equal, choose the better player. The maneuverability and acuteness of a player should be taken into account.

For the most part, a Wall bet is not a particularly good bet. If none of the players seems to have a good hand, check to see how many Jokers are available for picking. When the Walls are holding most of the Jokers, chances are someone will make Mah Jongg. Of course, it is a guess as to who will pick those Jokers, but once they are gotten, the hands will rapidly change. When the new card first comes out, and all players are struggling to learn the new hands, a Wall bet becomes more advisable. Also, a game with all inexperienced players favors a Wall bet when each one is holding a poor hand. The novice, even with Jokers, will still find it difficult to complete a hand to Mah Jongg.

The amount you will collect from winning a Wall bet should also be taken into consideration. You may prefer to gamble on a player making Mah Jongg where the profits would be far greater than the meager return from a Wall bet.

It should be an obligation on the part of the bettor to show the better if a correct bet has been made, instead of making the statement, "I bet correctly," and leave it at that.

Although every set is equipped with a better, if it becomes inoperable or gets lost, it can easily be replaced with pencil and paper. The bettor can write the name of the one holding the probable winning hand, which can be shown to all at the end of the game.

When a game ends, East becomes the next

bettor while the former bettor sits in East's seat. The next player to be East is the one who was sitting to the right of East. The process continues so that each player has a turn betting. In a six-handed game, where there are two bettors, each of them stays out for two consecutive games.

VIII

Rules and Regulations

"He who is conscious of what he lacks, and never forgets what he has already learned, may indeed be called learned."
—*Confucius*

There are many rules which govern correct play of the Mah Jongg game. Strict adherence should be made to all.

1. If, during the Charleston, it is discovered that one or more players have too many or too few tiles, all players throw in their hands and there is a reshuffle.

2. If a player has too many or too few tiles during the course of the play, that player is declared "dead" and ceases to play. The dead hand remains on the player's rack while the other three players continue the game. The dead player must

pay the winner and bettor(s) (if a correct bet was made).

3. If two players find they have too many or too few tiles during the game, both of them are declared dead, and they may not continue playing. The remaining two players continue, and if there is a winner between them, all players pay for the winning hand. If the bettor made the right bet, bettor is also paid by all players.

4. If three players are declared dead, the remaining player collects four times the value of the intact hand from the player who was the last to be declared dead.

5. If a player is declared dead and had been playing an Exposed hand, the Joker(s) in the correctly called exposure(s) *before* the error may be exchanged by the one holding the replacement tile.

6. If a player is declared dead and had been playing a Concealed hand, none of the Jokers contained therein can be exchanged.

7. If a player declares Mah Jongg in error, that player may continue playing only if declaration of Mah Jongg is retracted before the hand is displayed, and only if none of the other players has tossed in his/her hand. If the mistaken Mah Jongg

declarer displays hand and another player discards hand, the two remaining players continue the game. Everyone pays the resulting winner. If a third player mistakenly displays hand, the game ends and only the erring declarer is penalized. The amount paid to player whose hand remains intact is double the value of erring declarer's hand.

8. If an incorrect exposure is made, that player may be declared dead by any of the other players at any time during the course of the game (with the exclusion of the bettor, who must remain silent). If the incorrect exposure goes unnoticed, the erring player need not call it to anyone's attention and may continue playing. An incorrect exposure could be:

   a. a Kong when it should have been a Pung or Quint.
   b. a Pung when it should have been a Quint or Kong.
   c. a Quint when it should have been a Kong or Pung.
   d. an incorrect suit.
   e. th wrong set of Dragons.
   f. part of a Concealed hand (which can never be exposed).

   Sometimes, one exposure may appear to be proper initially. When two or more exposures have been made by the same player, a dead hand becomes more discernible because one could possibly figure out what hand is being played. It can then be realized that these exposures do not apply to any hand on the card.

9. If Mah Jongg is declared in error, that hand becomes dead once the tiles are displayed. The Jokers contained within the concealed portion of the hand may not be replaced. If an exposure was made with a Joker before the hand was declared dead, that Joker can still be claimed.

10. When a Concealed hand is displayed for Mah Jongg and it is realized that the hand is incorrect, none of the Jokers from this rack can be claimed.

11. In any exposure where there are Jokers, including that of a dead hand, the player whose turn it is may obtain the Jokers by replacing them with the exact tiles the Jokers represented.

12. Once a tile is discarded, it cannot be retracted to use for a Joker exchange.

13. If an exposure is made, it may be altered by the player before a discard is thrown. Once a player throws and declares a tile, the exposure cannot be touched.

14. A Joker must be in your hand before it can be used to call a tile for an exposure. When a Joker is exchanged, it can no longer be used to call a tile which was declared *before* the exchange was made. For example, your hand requires three Wests; you have only one. You cannot call a declared West, then make a Joker exchange, and expose *that* Joker with the two Wests. You can, however, call the third West if you already have two in your hand and *then* exchange a tile for a Joker to be used *later*.

15. A player may not call a tile for Mah Jongg and then replace a Joker. Declaring Mah Jongg ends the game and no play can follow the declaration.

16. When two like tiles are thrown and declared in rapid succession, the second tile is the one to be taken if there is a call for exposure or Mah Jongg. In a case where the second tile is a Joker, the call must be made with the face tile.

17. The bettor can never declare a player's hand dead.

18. The better must be shown when a correct bet has been made.

19. The bettor cannot disclose bet until the end of a game. To do so cancels the bet.

20. Once a player has thrown and declared a discard, he/she cannot call any tile that was thrown *before* his/her turn.

21. After a player has discarded, player cannot replace an exposed Joker. The discard ends turn and no play can be made until the next turn.

22. The player attempting a Jokerless hand must discard all Jokers. The Joker is declared by the name of the previously thrown tile. If the declared tile is called for exposure, the face tile (not the Joker) is taken.

IX

Viable Variations

"Do not preach what you practice until you have practiced what you teach."

—*Confucius*

The many variations found are really table rules. Defensive playing is an important aspect of the game, but how defensively a player is *permitted* to play is determined by the particular group playing.

In some games, you will find that the last twenty tiles (ten stacks) are called a "Hot Wall." As soon as a player is ready to pick the first tile from the Hot Wall, no one is permitted to throw what is considered to be a "hot" tile. Flowers are always hot at this time, and you are not allowed to throw one. Also, a tile is considered to be hot if you cannot account for three of the same. The three tiles could either be in your hand, on the table, in an exposure, or a combination of all. However, you may play in a group that will allow a hot tile to be thrown—*but*—if you do throw one and it produces

97

Mah Jongg for someone, you are penalized. The penalty may vary from paying a set amount to the winner to paying the winner the full amount that would have been collected from each player. The latter is a stiff penalty and would discourage most players from throwing a hot tile.

In Figure 63, you can see the last five stacks (as a result of the Wall being broken initially at five) separated from five stacks which are taken from the Wall of Player No. 2. Combined, they form the Hot Wall.

You may find yourself playing in a game where a "Cold Wall" is set up. When there is a Cold Wall, it pertains to the last ten stacks (twenty tiles), as did the Hot Wall above. As soon as you reach the last ten stacks, no player is permitted to *call* a tile for Mah Jongg. At this point, player must *pick* the tile from the Cold Wall to produce Mah Jongg. A call for *exposure*, however, may be made in the Cold Wall.

In yet another game, you may find both Hot and Cold Walls set up. The Cold Wall refers to the last ten stacks, and the Hot Wall is the ten stacks preceding. (Refer to Figure 63 to see how the separations for the Hot and Cold Walls are made.) The method of play for the Hot and Cold Walls is the same as when each is found separately in a game.

There will be times when you will play in an

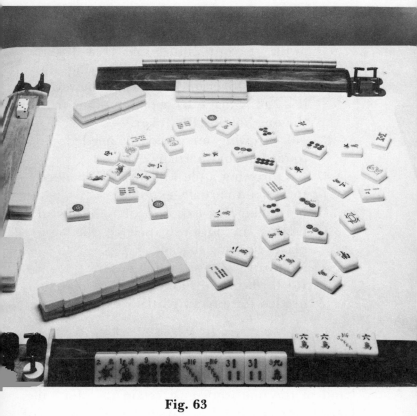

Fig. 63

extremely defensive game. You will not be permitted to do many, if any, of the following:

1. No passing of Jokers. In a game where you pick and look ahead, you cannot call a tile if your future tile is a Joker. (Calling would necessitate passing the Joker.) A Joker must be passed, however, if a call is made by a player other than the one holding the Joker.
2. No throwing an obviously needed tile toward a hand partially exposed.
3. No throwing a tile which *may* be needed for a hand partially exposed.
4. No calling for exposure if it results in passing an obviously needed tile to a player needing that tile.
5. No throwing to a third exposure.
6. No throwing of Flowers if they may be needed for a hand partially exposed.

If an obviously needed tile is thrown inadvertently, that player is required to take the tile back, rack it, and throw another. This will, at times, ruin the hand of the one who must retain the "hot" tile. Once a player's hand is inoperable as a result of enforced defensive playing, each tile thrown thereafter should be one that is not needed by the other players. This is not always able to be determined, but a likely safe throw would be the third of a particular tile (the *third* Three Dot or the *third* Green or the *third* West, etc.). A Flower should certainly not be thrown at this point.

If a player calls a tile and exposes a Pung, Kong or Quint with one or more Jokers, the Joker(s) may be exchanged with the face tile(s) for which intended. The player making the replacement(s) must wait until turn before the exchange(s) can be made. The Joker(s) remain(s) on the rack of the one who made the exchange(s), who may then use the Joker(s) for any other tile(s). Once the original exposure contains only face tiles, all the Jokers having been replaced, that hand can become a Jokerless hand. This play would be classified as a table rule, and must be set up as such before the game begins.

At the end of the Charleston, after the Optional pass has been exchanged, each of the four players may place one, two or three unneeded tiles face down in the center of the table. East shuffles all the tiles and is first to pick the same number of tiles put in. The second player picks next, then the third, followed by the fourth, each replacing the number of tiles just discarded. This play is a table rule called "Garbage." It is an extra way of obtaining a needed tile or retrieving a tile that had to be passed during the Across. However, it is possible to pick up the same tiles originally put into the Garbage.

The rules set up by the National Mah Jongg

League state that there should be no picking or looking ahead. What this means is that no player may see a future tile until his/her turn to pick. The steps are:

1. East discards the fourteenth tile, one that is not needed.
2. Player No. 2 picks the next tile from the Wall. If the tile is needed, No. 2 places it on rack and a tile which is unwanted is thrown and declared. If No. 2 does not need the picked tile, it is thrown and declared.
3. Player No. 3 does the same as the two preceding players, followed by Player No. 4.

In each case, a player picks a tile only upon turn. An evaluation is made whether or not to keep the tile, and one that is not wanted is thrown and declared. If the declared tile is needed by another player, it may be called to complete a Pung, Kong or Quint in an Exposed hand; or it may be called to complete Mah Jongg in an Exposed or Concealed hand. If the tile is called for exposure, it is passed to the one calling it, and it then becomes that player's turn to discard. If the declared tile is called for Mah Jongg, there are no more turns for anyone. The game ceases when someone has Mah Jongg.

The above does make for a slower game, and many players have gotten away from this ruling. Instead, as soon as a player throws a tile it could immediately be replaced with another picked tile. This newly picked tile is called the Future, and it is the identical tile which would have been picked by that player if picking and looking ahead were not permitted. Technically, this tile does not belong to the player until it is the player's turn to play again. Therefore, the future must be held and cannot be put into the rack *until player's next turn*. If a tile is called, all futures must be passed away, even if a player needs the future he/she is holding. When there are no calls, the needed tile may be placed into the rack upon the player's turn, *not before*.

Futures are passed in the following manner:

1. If East were to call a tile thrown by Player No. 3, No. 3 would pass his/her tile to East and would receive East's tile in return. Players No. 2 and No. 4 would exchange tiles.
2. If East were to call a tile thrown by Player No. 2, No. 2 would pass his/her tile to East; East would follow by passing his/her tile to No. 4; No. 4 would pass to No. 3; and No. 3 would pass to No. 2.
3. If East were to call a tile thrown by Player No. 4, No. 4 would pass the called tile to East; East would pass his/her tile to

No. 2; No. 2 would pass his/her tile to
No. 3; and No. 3 would pass his/her tile
to No. 4.

In other words, when a call is made the called
tile is passed *to* the one making the call and all
other players follow the same direction of passing.
Any player who plays an Exposed hand may call a
tile for exposure if it completes a Pung, Kong or
Quint. The passing of futures would be the same
procedure as above. (See Figure 64 to facilitate the
explanation for passing of futures.)

In a game where the players do pick and look
ahead of their turn, futures should be held on top
of the rack, care being taken not to show it. It
cannot be stressed enough that this future does
not belong to the player until it is player's turn;
therefore, it cannot be racked until player's turn.
Slipping a tile onto the end of the rack before the
actual turn should not be allowed. As long as the
future is held on top of the rack and not in it, there
can never be a problem of not knowing which tile
should be passed in case a call is made.

In some games where there is no looking ahead
at futures, the players are permitted to *pick* the
future immediately after they discard, but are not
permitted to *look* at it until it is their turn to play
again. Upon the player's turn, the future may then
be seen, decided upon, racked if needed, thrown if
not.

East

Player #4

Player #2

Player #3

Fig. 64

TWO-HANDED MAH JONGG: The Walls are built as they are for four hands. The two players sit opposite one another, and they take turns being East. The tiles are picked the same way as usual, but the Charleston is eliminated. Play begins with East, who throws and declares the first tile.

THREE-HANDED MAH JONGG: It is played exactly as a two-handed game (as above).

X

Timely Tips

"Man may be deceived but cannot be led astray."
                                        —_Confucius_

Try to make Mah Jongg by _picking_ the fourteenth
tile to complete your hand, rather than by calling
it. You are paid double the amount by all players
when the last tile you need is picked by you,
yourself. If a declared tile would give you Mah
Jongg, there may be times when you would prefer
to wait awhile to see if you could pick that tile
yourself. You might take the chance to wait if you
could utilize more than one particular tile to make
Mah Jongg. Also, if it is early in the game, you
could wait awhile longer to see if you are able to
pick your Mah Jongg. You would do this only if
the tile (or tiles) you need is not already on the
table. Don't hesitate to call a tile for Mah Jongg if it
is the last available one. In other words, do not
pass up a call when the alternative is the need to
pick a Joker.

While you are still in the learning stage, attempt to complete the simplest hand in the quickest way. For the experienced player, there will be times when the opportunity to gamble will present itself. For instance, if you are on a winning streak and you feel "hot," you might even discard Mah Jongg in an attempt to make a more expensive hand. This could be done if it is early in the game and you made sure that the needed tiles have not already been declared. If you held several Jokers and the hand could easily be switched so you would not need more than two additional tiles, it might behoove you to gamble a bit. There is definitely something to be said about streaks. You will find there are some days that you can't do anything wrong. There will be others when no matter what you do, the results will be disastrous. Capitalize on your up-cycle. Take chances, but do it wisely. When things do not appear to be going your way, be more conservative.

During the Charleston, be observant of the passes you receive. You can often determine the type of hand a player is attempting simply from the passes you get. For instance, if you receive two Lefts comprised of all odd numbers, it is almost a certainty the player to your right needs the even numbers. When you realize this, be cognizant of your pass to that player. In this case, you would try to be deliberate about passing anything but evens.

If you can prevent it, do not pass a pair, and

certainly not a triple, during the Charleston. It could surely better your opponent's hand, and you don't want to do this. Try to mix up the tiles you pass, if possible. If you have a choice, pass tiles that do not particularly go together. A Wind, a Dragon and an odd number, or any three tiles which do not mesh, is the type of pass you should make. You would not, however, pass one of your needed tiles just to break up a good pass. This would be too defensive. A Flower is generally an advantageous tile because most of the hands require at least two Flowers. If possible, do not pass them. It is wiser to pass one of your own beneficial tiles rather than to pass a pair of Flowers. If you anticipate that you may have to pass one of the tiles you will need yourself, do it on the First Left. There would be a good chance, then, for you to get it back on the Last Across.

Watch the discards as the game is in progress. From them, you will get the knack of determining the type of hand each player is attempting. If you suspect a player needs the Winds, throw them early in the game if you do not need them for your own hand. Chances are the player needing the Winds is not ready to make a call, and it is possible for you to kill that hand before it even has a chance to get started. Concentrate on completing your own hand, and at the same time make a conscious effort to destroy your adversaries'.

Discard early the tiles you suspect another to

need. You can often tell by the passes you received during the Charleston what tiles are needed by others. If Dragons were initially passed and they do not come back to you during the passing, you will know they are being used by someone. If you should pick a Dragon during the beginning of the game, it is wise to throw it immediately. Often, the one needing the Dragons will not be set up early in the game to make the call. And, if not, the Dragon you throw will become dead, making it more difficult for that player to complete the hand. Also, if the Dragons are needed for a Concealed hand, it is most unlikely for the player to be set for Mah Jongg early. Again, when you declare a Dragon, the percentages for completing a Dragon hand will lessen. If a number tile is called, it is pretty impossible to determine which hand the player is attempting. When two exposures have been made, the hand becomes more discernible. At this point, you may choose to play more defensively, especially if you feel your chances to make Mah Jongg are nil. You would then hold back the obviously needed tiles. If your chances for Mah Jongg are good, do not be concerned with throwing the hot tiles you may pick. I have found it more advantageous to play gutsy (when I have a good hand) than to play scared.

Although you will try to prevent it, you will occasionally pass matching tiles during the Charleston. Matching tiles are not necessarily a pair or triple. It could be two or three tiles toward a particular hand. If they are retained by the one to whom you made this pass, make sure you do not pass similar tiles when passing to this player again. Some may say you are cheating if you watch to see which tiles you pass during the Charleston are placed into your opponent's hand. Being *aware* is certainly not classified as cheating. When you notice, for instance, that a pass of three Winds are put into the opposition's rack, it would be most unwise to pass a similar set of tiles to that player. As a matter of fact, when you know someone is saving the Winds, if it is at all possible, hold back as many Winds as you can during the Charleston without destroying your own hand. Do not break up your own possibilities to do this, but very often you will have enough stray tiles to pass without deliberately handing over what you know will be needed. Passing defensively is as important as playing defensively.

When you call a tile and then expose the Pung, Kong or Quint with Jokers, remember that your opponents can take these Jokers for themselves if they can replace them with the tiles they are meant to be. Be aware that these Joker replacements can become valuable weapons in your opponents' hands. If you have passed a Three Dot, for instance, due to a call, naturally you will know who is holding that tile. If it is racked and you need it for your hand, it would not be wise for you to call a

Three Dot that is thrown by another player if it has to be exposed with a Joker. The reason is, the one to whom you passed the original Three Dot would then have the opportunity of replacing it, and would then use that Joker for his/her hand. What happens often is that once the first Three Dot falls, shortly thereafter the next one will be thrown. Then you can call it.

There will be times when you will be tempted to call a tile for a Kong even though you will have to expose three Jokers in order to do so. Most of the time, this would not be a smart play. However, if this exposure will put you on call, do it. You must realize that by doing this, anyone holding the tiles for which you have used the Jokers may replace them. The Jokers that become part of your opponents' hands will certainly better their hands, and if all three Jokers are taken by the same player, that player's hand has to improve considerably. If you are calling a tile and must expose three Jokers, *but* two or three of those tiles have already been declared and are dead on the table, you are not risking much by the call. Consider this when you are exposing two or three Jokers. Although you are always trying to better your own hand, you are not interested in improving your adversaries'.

Whenever you call a tile, you are giving the other players information about your hand. For instance, when you call a Wind, it will be known that you need other Winds. Your opponents may then play defensively and try to prevent you from getting your needed tiles. It is a good play, therefore, not to call the first Wind thrown. Perhaps you may pick it yourself. If, however, another such Wind should fall, then you must call it. Call the first declared Wind only if that tile will set you.

When you pick up your initial thirteen tiles and find that you are holding two or more Jokers, try to play a hand that requires more single numbers and pairs rather than a hand that needs Pungs and Kongs. This type of hand is relatively easy to complete when you begin with Jokers. The reason is that the Jokers become very interchangeable. Whenever a needed face tile is picked, the Jokers can serve in another position. This kind of hand will rarely become dead because the Jokers you have will back up the missing tiles.

If your hand becomes dead, by all means play defensively. Do not throw any tile you suspect another to need. Break up your hand and begin to throw your own tiles. Check the table and throw safe tiles only, if this is possible. Don't be lazy. If you can't possibly make a hand, don't let anyone else make one either.

If the hand you are attempting becomes dead, try to switch it to another hand. When you can, keep tiles on reserve for switching. The experienced player will have several hands in mind, and when one hand fails to materialize, another one should be waiting in the wings.

113

There will be times when your chances to make Mah Jongg are next to impossible. Push a hand by calling. Then try to work around this call. You will be achieving two things by doing this. First, there may be some remote chance that you could pick lucky and a possibility to make Mah Jongg could develop after all. It is always more fun to make an attempt than to sit back and give up. Secondly, by making a call, you will put your opponents more on the defensive, and this could result in spoiling their hands. If you are able to call a second time, you are apt to lessen the chances of your opponents' Mah Jongg because of their concern about you. Remember, no one can see the tiles you are holding, and once you have shown two exposures, some players may break up their own hands just to prevent having to throw another tile to you.

As a result of different happenings, you will occasionally know that a particular tile will be called by someone if it is discarded. If you pick that tile and don't need it for your hand, you have two options. You could either throw it immediately or perhaps you could hold it with the hope of finding a more strategic time for discarding it. For instance, in a game where you pick and look at your future tile ahead of your actual turn, you will sometimes be required to pass a Joker due to a call being made by another player. If you had to pass the Joker to the player needing the tile you previously racked "for the opportune moment,"

114

this would be the perfect time to throw it. The player needing the tile could not call it because of the Joker being held. So, although this opponent has gained a Joker, at the same time a needed face tile would be lost. This discard would be a very good defensive maneuver on your part.

Different players have different mannerisms. When you are observant, you will see things that are done which can be beneficial to you. For example, you may be able to determine how close someone is to Mah Jongg. Some players separate the intact hand from the tiles which are extraneous. You will always know when these players are two from set, on call, etc. Prevent this from happening to you. Don't give anyone the opportunity of "reading" your hand. Always keep your tiles together; have no gaps.

When you play with the same people over a period of time, you will notice different things each one will do. You may find someone who generally picks and throws tiles with the right hand, switching to the left hand when on call. Some may cry about how bad their hand is when they actually have a very good one. At times players will make a "Freudian slip," miscalling a tile they have thrown, declaring it as the tile they are waiting to claim. Capitalize on "reading" the opponents' gestures, and conversely, realize that your opponents may be trying to read yours.

In a game where picking and looking ahead is

permitted, do not separate the tiles on your rack when you pick a tile you need. By making room for the needed tile before it is your turn to play, you are signaling your opponents of what transpired. If another player were contemplating a call, it would certainly be made in an attempt to rid you of the tile you were holding. As a result of the call, you would have to pass your future tile. This would be a good defensive move on the part of your opponent. Always keep your tiles together and don't give unnecessary information by doing otherwise.

Some players turn their tile upside down after another of the same has been thrown and declared. It is their way of keeping track of dead tiles as they fall. At the same time, however, the observant player can keep track of the opponents' needs by mentally noting when a tile is upturned. If the same tile is thrown a second time, some players turn their identical tile on its side. Again, this is a signal for the observant opposition. When you see a player turning over a tile that was just declared, you will know what tile that player needs. If you should happen to have that tile in your own hand and don't need it, it would be wise to throw it on your next turn. Chances are your opponent was unable to call the first or second one thrown, and by throwing another of the same quickly, you could be injuring the hand of the opposition. When a player turns down several tiles after the

116

identical ones have been thrown and declared, it will become more apparent what type of hand that opponent is attempting. If you were to realize that this player is attempting a 3-6-9 hand, for instance, your best move would be to continually throw those numbers—provided, of course, you do not need them for your own hand.

You should get into the habit of placing the tiles you receive during the Charleston on your rack automatically, whether you need them or not. Then, you can juggle around the tiles you may need without your opponents observing just which ones you retain. Remember, just as you will be able to determine players' hands at times, they too will be able to assess yours if you are not careful.

Don't get into the habit of making similar passes on the First Right. Some players prefer not to go for a Wind hand, and will invariably pass at least one Wind on the First Right. If you are labeled as one who always passes Winds, the one to receive your First Right will anticipate this. You are giving that player an edge. If the player has any doubt whatever (and there almost always is doubt about the initial pass), you can be sure the Winds will be saved knowing that you will be passing them. Vary your passes, especially on the First Right and on the First and Second Left.

If a player stops the Charleston after the First Left, it would be a foolish move for the one sitting opposite to allow an Optional pass. If the

Charleston is stopped midway, you can be sure that player has a pretty good hand. Don't give the one who stopped the Charleston the chance of obtaining any more needed tiles by passing an Optional. Stand pat—even at the expense of your own hand.

When you are attempting an Exposed hand and are all set to call for each Pung, Kong or Quint you may need after the First Left, a good defensive move would be to stop the Charleston. You may have three tiles to pass which you don't need and could continue the Charleston, but don't do it. To do so could improve the others' hands while you would be making very little change with your own. After the First Left, few players ever have much of a hand. Don't give them the chance to better it by continuing the passing. The tile or tiles you would receive during subsequent passes will eventually be thrown, and you can retrieve them by calling.

Do reverse mannerisms to confuse your opponents. If you are in the habit of picking tiles with one hand until you are on call, then begin to pick with the other hand, eventually those playing with you will know when you are indeed on call. Switch your "picking hand" at times when you are not on call. By confusing observant players, they will attempt to play more defensively—be afraid to throw a tile they think you will need. At times, they may even destroy their own possibilities while trying to prevent you from making a hand. They are less apt to complete their own hands the more they worry about you.

Don't always rack your tiles the same way. For instance, you will find most players keep Flowers to the extreme left of their rack and discards to the extreme right. When you know this to be true of a particular player, you will always know when Flowers are being held. Whatever information you can derive about another player's hand will most certainly assist you in one way or another. If you know that a particular tile is needed for Mah Jongg by one of the players, you would never throw it. If you know a player needs a tile, but are unsure if it would give that player Mah Jongg or not, you might take the chance of throwing it *if* you had a good hand yourself. If you had a poor hand, with perhaps no chance of bettering it, you would probably decide to play defensively and would not throw this needed tile. Try to "read" your opponents at all times, but make sure they are unable to "read" you.

I have found that it is to your advantage to call the tiles you need early in the game (with the exception of Winds, as explained earlier in this chapter). Many conservative players wait until the tile they need has fallen twice before they will call and expose a Joker with the Kong or Pung. They are afraid that another player will replace the Joker, so they wait to see if they can pick the tile themselves. It is true that the Joker may be

119

replaced by another player, but it is also possible for you to pick that tile, and then you could replace the Joker yourself. You have the same chance as the others to pick the Joker replacement.

To capsulize the foregoing poignant pointers:

1. Capitalize on your up-cycle. Be gutsy when you are "hot," conservative when you are not.

2. Don't pass matching tiles during the Charleston.

3. Discard early the tiles you suspect another to need.

4. Pass defensively.

5. Thought should be given before making a call that would require exposing two or three Jokers.

6. Attempt a hand requiring single numbers or pairs if you open with two or more Jokers.

7. When you can't make a hand, play extremely defensively.

8. Push a hand by calling.

9. Learn to "read" your opponents' mannerisms.

10. Do not exchange an Optional with a player who stops the Charleston.

11. Stop the Charleston after the First Left if you are set to call remaining needed tiles—even if you do have three tiles with which to continue passing.

XI

Check the Cheat

"A man who has committed a mistake and doesn't correct it, is committing another mistake."

—*Confucius*

This chapter is not intended to instruct the cheat. On the contrary, its purpose is to make the players aware of what can happen during a game, and the safeguards against it. I, personally, have played in several different games and was conscious of "infractions" being made. The range was from slight to extreme.

The most common "problem" I have encountered occurs when a call is made. The difficulty prevails in a game where the players pick and look at their "future" (the fourteenth tile which is picked from the Wall) before their actual turn to play. Although this kind of game is much faster, and therefore more enjoyable to the experienced player, it does create havoc at times.

When a declared tile is called for exposure, each and every player must pass his/her future. There are times when a player would like to retain that future, and this is when the temptation sets in to do just that. Some players will rack their future (put the tile into their hands) before it is their turn to play. This should never be done. First of all, the future does not belong to the player until it is his/her turn. Therefore, it *cannot* be racked ahead of turn. Secondly, if a tile is called, the racked tile will have to be passed. There will be times when a player will legitimately forget just which tile was racked, and possibly the wrong tile will be passed. There will be other times when the racked tile will not be passed because the player *chooses* not to pass it. During the play of the game, while all players are deeply engrossed in their own hands, it is very easy to slip out a tile which a player does not need and pass that one in place of the actual future.

To avoid any confusion, and especially to avoid the intentional racking of tiles before each player's turn, it should be common practice by all players to hold the future. Or, it can be set down on *top* of the rack (where an exposure would be put) without exposing it. When it is player's turn, it can then be racked or thrown, at player's discretion. No one should be given the temptation to rack and keep a tile prior to turn. The problem can be avoided by setting the rule of not allowing futures to be racked until it is the player's turn.

*   *   *   *

122

Check the Cheat

Another difficulty which can arise in a game where picking and looking ahead is permitted is when a player calls a tile "two back" (the tile before the last declared tile). For instance, East has a right to call the tile thrown by Player No. 3 even if Player No. 4 has already racked future and has thrown another tile. (It should be noted that calling two back is only permitted in a game where there is picking and looking ahead.) When East calls the tile two back, Player No. 4 must then remove the racked tile and pass it along with his/her next future. *Both* tiles must be passed. (They become the recipient's first and second futures, to be used in the same order had there been no call.) Once a tile is racked, the player will sometimes forget just which tile it was. Sometimes the "forgetting" is intentional. Be observant. Try to see just where a racked tile is being placed. Then, if a call is made, you will know exactly which tile should be passed. If a player forgets, you can help him/her remember.

*   *   *   *

During the play of picking and throwing tiles, it is not uncommon for a tile to be miscalled. Most of the time, it is due to an oversight. However, it does happen that a miscalled tile is deliberate. Because the play is so rapid in a game where the players pick and look at their tile ahead of their actual turn, the miscalled tile can go unnoticed. Whether this is done accidentally or intentionally, the result is the same. A player could possibly lose a needed tile unless the error is discovered immediately. It is difficult to watch each and every tile thrown, but it is not a bad idea to occasionally spot-check a declared tile. A player who is listening for a particular tile, who does not hear it declared, and then sees it on the table at the end of the game would be the one to realize that a tile was miscalled. If this happens too often, it is advisable to play the game one way only—do not allow a tile to be picked until it is the player's turn. In other words, no advance picking. In that way, each declared tile can be scrutinized and there would be no chance of a tile being miscalled.

* * * *

It is good practice to check a player's hand for Mah Jongg when it is declared. Do not throw in your hand just because you've heard a player say "Mah Jongg." Many errors can be, and are, made in completing the hand. Do not pay the winner unless you can account for every tile in that hand, making sure that exactly fourteen tiles have been utilized and that the hand is an exact duplicate of the one shown on the card. Mistakes can happen. A player may think he/she has Mah Jongg, but may be short one tile. Unless you check the hand carefully, one less tile is not always detectable. Especially when the Mah Jongg declarer has several Jokers in the hand, it is often difficult to see at a glance that an error has been made. Another common mistake is for the player to have mismatched the Dragons with the numbers, or to have a Pung where there should have been a Kong (or vice versa). Accidents do happen, but if it is spotted immediately each time it occurs, the "accidents" will not become chronic.

*   *   *   *

During the Charleston, there are two times when tiles may be stolen—on the First Left and on the Final Right. As you have learned in the chapter "Challenging Charleston," the stolen tile must be passed once the decision to steal it has been made. The player is, however, entitled to look at the stolen tile, but must pass it regardless of whether it is needed or not. Occasionally, the player doing the stealing may want to retain the tile that was about to be stolen. It could be looked at quickly prior to stealing, and another tile could be stolen instead. When a player is going to steal, be observant. Make sure that the first tile looked at is the actual tile passed.

*   *   *   *

If a better is being used, it is possible for the wrong number to be dialed. Therefore, when there is a bettor involved, the bets made should be verified. The bettor is not permitted to reveal the bet before the end of the game, but the better should be shown *after* Mah Jongg has been made. The bettor is not allowed to help any player during the play. It is obvious that any information divulged by the bettor would aid a player; therefore, there should be no coaching on the part of the bettor. Once the better has been dialed for the bet, it cannot be touched until the end of the game. It has happened that a poor hand was bet on in error, and miraculously, the hand was completed for Mah Jongg. The bettor was paid for the winning bet, even though the mistake was made. It is a good ruling to have the bet stand, whether a mistake was made or not—win or lose. Even if the bet is made by mistake, if the winner's number is on the better, the bettor should be paid and, conversely, if the winner's number is *not* on the better, the bettor should *not* be paid even if he/she *intended* to bet correctly.

*   *   *   *

There may be times when two players get together before the game and decide to be partners. Since they will pool their winnings, it doesn't matter just which one of the two comes out winning—as long as one of the partners does win. When tiles are being passed during the Charleston, one partner can "feed" the other with especially good passes. This could easily go undetected in a four-handed game. If there is a bettor, it could never happen because feeding would be spotted by the onlooker. It is advisable, therefore, to have the players rotate their seats around East every fourth game in a four-handed game. At least this would help to break up some of the flow of passing from one individual to another.

*　　*　　*　　*

It is very important for East to roll the dice and Break the Wall according to this roll before the players pick their initial tiles. Some games have a table rule of automatically Breaking the Wall at ten, and eliminating the roll of the dice completely. They claim that this procedure saves time, and I suppose it does save a little. However, the time saved is not worth the difficulty which can ensue.

I, personally, was involved with a game for several months before I realized how one of the players was cheating. As a result of the Wall being broken consistently at ten, it can be figured out just which tiles a player will pick no matter who is East at the time or where the player happens to sit. I grant you, it takes a lot of figuring, but it can be done—and was done.

Jokers, because they can replace any face tile (except for the few Jokerless hands), are considered to be the most valuable tiles. Having Jokers facilitates making Mah Jongg. This being the case, it behooved the cheat to *set up* the Wall, placing several Jokers in the stacks from which she would pick. Her moves began when a game ended and all the tiles were face up on the table. As the tiles were being turned over by all players, readying them for the shuffle, the cheat palmed some Jokers. While we were all conversing, not paying attention or suspecting what was taking place, a minimum of two Jokers remained beneath the cheat's hands. She was very deft at building the Wall and would complete hers rapidly . . . especially if she had to "work on" another player's Wall. She would stack the Jokers into the Wall from which she would pick as she would "help" that player build the Wall. The times her picks came from her own Wall, she simply planted the Jokers there with ease. No one suspected—it was all so easy.

This all could have been avoided if we simply enforced the rule of rolling the dice before East's Wall was broken, rather than always Breaking the Wall at ten.

*   *   *   *

Instead of surreptitiously checking the better to see if the correct bet was made, the bettor should automatically display the better at the end of the game. The bet can then be verified by all, and there can never be any doubt in anyone's mind if, indeed, the bettor was paid unnecessarily.

*   *   *   *

Never assume that these things could not happen in your game. You never know what provokes someone to commit the infraction. Some people *must* win—at all costs. There are some who feel important, or more intelligent, or better than the next, if they generally come out winning. There are others who simply cannot afford to lose. Don't let these things happen in your game, especially since you can safeguard against them.

XII

Quaich of Queries

"Do not worry about people not knowing your ability, but worry if you have not got it."

—*Confucius*

Q. Is it foolish to throw Mah Jongg away in favor of going for a more expensive hand?

A. For the most part, yes. If you have Mah Jongg, declare it. At times, however, when you are running particularly lucky, you may want to gamble and take a chance to win a bigger (more expensive) hand. But bear in mind that a small win is better than no win at all.

Q. Should a player always replace a Joker with the face tile the Joker represents?

A. If you are not going for a Jokerless hand, exchange the Joker with the face tile. Do not give another player the opportunity to retrieve a valuable tile (the Joker). If you *are*

131

going for a Jokerless hand, replacing a Joker with one of the tiles you need for your own hand would lessen your possibilities for Mah Jongg. Therefore, this would be a poor play.

Q. Can a player have Mah Jongg after the Charleston?

A. The only one who could possibly make Mah Jongg after the Charleston is East. The reason is, Mah Jongg requires the utilization of fourteen tiles, and only East would have this number of tiles after the Charleston.

Q. Does any money exchange hands when there is a Wall game?

A. If the Bettor bets on the Wall and a Wall game results, each player pays the Bettor for making the correct bet. When there is no Bettor, no money exchanges hands after a Wall game.

Q. Can two people have Mah Jongg at the same time?

A. Only in a game where "picking and looking ahead" is permitted could two people have Mah Jongg simultaneously. However, the official winner is the one whose turn comes first.

Q. Would both players be paid if they each had Mah Jongg?

A. No. Only the player whose turn was first would be paid. The other person holding Mah Jongg would also have to pay the official winner.

Q. What happens if a tile has been incorrectly declared?

A. If it is discovered immediately that a tile was incorrectly named, the proper name is announced. Anyone needing the correctly declared tile may call it. If a mistake in declaring a tile is discovered later in the game, nothing more than calling the error to everyone's attention can be done. Unfortunately, it can no longer be called for Mah Jongg or exposure.

Q. If a player declares Mah Jongg and claims to have made a 20¢ hand, which has been verified by all, then realizes the same fourteen tiles could be used for a more expensive hand, what price is paid to the winner?

A. Once a hand is established, the winner collects for the value of the original hand.

Q. If a tile is thrown and declared, can player retract it?

A. No. Once a tile has been discarded, it must remain on the table—unless it is called by one of the other players.

Q. Can a discarded Joker be claimed by any of the players?

A. No. When a Joker is discarded, it is declared the name of the previously thrown tile. If that tile is needed, only the face tile can be called. The Joker always remains on the table.

Q. How many Jokers can be replaced at one time?

A. You may take as many Jokers as you want, as long as you have the proper face tiles with which to replace them.

Q. If a Pung is exposed, can it be changed into a Kong?

A. When an exposure is made, it can only be changed prior to discarding. Once you throw and declare a tile, the exposure must remain as is.

Q. If two tiles are thrown in rapid succession, can they both be called simultaneously?

A. The first of the two tiles may be called by any of the players. If it is, the second tile to have been thrown has to be passed as a result of the call. If it is discarded once again, it can then be called; but never can two tiles be called and claimed simultaneously.

Q. What is the best way to learn the new card?

A. Since many of the old hands are repeated on the new card, there actually aren't too many new ones to memorize. Check off those hands which must be studied, and put your total concentration on those select few.

Q. When there is a Wall game, is that game replayed?
A. No. A Wall game marks the completion of a game, and the start of a new game follows.

Q. Is the bettor permitted to ask a player to point out the hand being attempted?
A. Technically, there is not supposed to be conversation between bettor and player. However, since many players do not arrange their tiles in very good order, it is often difficult for the bettor to know exactly what the player has in mind after the Charleston. Therefore, I think it is common courtesy for the bettor to be apprised of the player's intentions.

Q. Can a Joker be passed in the Charleston?
A. No, a Joker can never be passed during the Charleston.

Q. Can a player declare Mah Jongg and then exchange a tile for a Joker?

A. No. When a player declares Mah Jongg, all play ceases. There can be no more picking, discarding or exchanging of tiles.

Q. Can a player stop the Charleston even though that player has three tiles to pass?

A. Yes. The Charleston may be stopped by any player after the first three compulsory passes without giving any explanation for doing so.

Q. Can a discarded tile be called to complete a pair?

A. A discarded tile cannot be called to complete a pair for exposure. However, it can be called for Mah Jongg regardless of whether or not it completes a pair, Pung, Kong, etc.

XIII

Glorious Glossary

"Not to know words is to be without the fluid needful to understand."

—*Confucius*

ACROSS	One of the passes of the Charleston.
BAM	One of the three suits.
BETTER	A round, movable disc used for making bets.
BETTOR	The player temporarily out of the game who is making a bet.
BIG JOKER	Used as a "wild card" to replace any tile (except in a Jokerless hand). Also referred to as "Joker."
BLIND PASS	A pass of three tiles you *receive* and then use as your pass *to* another player. The decision to make this pass is made *before you see* the tiles, hence the term "blind pass."

BREAKING THE WALL	The stacks held back against East's rack until the final stages of the game. The number of stacks which remain is determined by the roll of the dice.
CALL	To claim a discarded tile for exposure or Mah Jongg.
CARD	The Mah Jongg card outlines the various hands which can be played.
CHARLESTON	The passing and exchange of tiles before the actual play begins.
CHIPS	Used in place of money.
COLD WALL	A table rule which requires the players to *pick* their Mah Jongg tile rather than being able to claim a discard for Mah Jongg during a specified time of the game.
CONCEALED HAND	Specified as such on the card. Tiles for this type of hand cannot be called unless it is a call for Mah Jongg.
COURTESY	The Optional pass during the Charleston.
COVERED	When a tile has been thrown and declared, it has "covered"

the previously thrown and declared tile.

CRAK One of the three suits.

CURTSY Pushing the Wall forward.

DEAD HAND Too few or too many tiles. Also, an improper exposure results in a dead hand.

DEAD TILE When a given tile can no longer be picked (because it is being utilized in another's exposure or due to it being previously thrown and declared).

DECLARE Stating the name of a discard.

DOGGING Holding back and intentionally not throwing a possibly needed tile.

DOT One of the three suits.

DRAGON Referring to the Red, White (or Soap) or Green.

EAST The first player. Also, one of the four Winds.

EXPOSED HAND Specified as such on the card. A tile may be called for exposure or Mah Jongg for this hand.

EXPOSURE The Pung, Kong or Quint which must be revealed after a tile is called.

FACE TILE Any tile other than a Joker.

FALL — A tile thrown and declared is a tile which has "fallen."

FINAL RIGHT — The last compulsory pass of the Charleston.

FIRST LEFT — The third pass of the Charleston.

FIRST RIGHT — The first pass of the Charleston.

FLOWER — One of the tiles needed to complete various hands.

FUTURE — The tile a player picks from the Wall in advance of turn.

GARBAGE — A table rule whereby superfluous tiles may be exchanged for other tiles at the conclusion of the Charleston.

GREEN — One of the three types of Dragons.

HAND — One of the many combinations of tiles which, when properly arranged, constitutes Mah Jongg.

HONORS — Referring to the Winds and/or Dragons.

HOT TILE — Strictly a table rule in some games when only particular tiles are permitted to be thrown. At that time, all others are considered "hot."

HOT WALL — A table rule which disallows

throwing hot tiles during a particular segment of the game.

JOKER   Used as a "wild card" to replace any tile. (Not permitted to be used in a Jokerless hand.) Also called "Big Joker."

KITTY   Money collected from each player to be used as a bonus. (This is a table rule.)

KONG   Four of a kind.

NORTH   One of the four Winds.

ON CALL   Ready for Mah Jongg. Also referred to as "set."

OPTIONAL   The last pass of the Charleston. This is not a compulsory pass.

PAT HAND   When every tile on the rack is needed for a particular hand.

PIE   A predetermined, maximum amount one can lose during a session.

PUNG   Three of a kind.

QUINT   Five of a kind.

RACK   Used to facilitate the viewing and manipulating of tiles which eventually become a hand. Also, against which the Walls are placed.

141

RACKING	Putting a tile into one's hand.
RED	One of the three Dragons.
SECOND LEFT	The fourth pass of the Charleston; it becomes compulsory provided that the Charleston has not been stopped after the first three passes.
SET	When a hand is ready for and needs only one more tile to complete Mah Jongg. Also referred to as "on call."
SOAP	One of the three Dragons. Also called "White."
SOUTH	One of the four Winds.
STACK	Two tiles, one on top of the other, both face down. Nineteen stacks against each of four racks comprise the Wall.
STEALING	Passing a tile (or tiles) on the First Left or Final Right of the Charleston, which is selected from the pass just *received* by player. Tile is chosen *before* it is seen by player "stealing" it.
THROW	To discard.
TILES	Rectangular pieces, each with engraved characters on one side and blank on the other.

142

WALL	The stacks of tiles placed face down against each of four racks.
WALL GAME	When a game has ended and there is no winner, it is said to have been a "Wall game."
WEST	One of the four Winds.
WHITE	One of the three Dragons. Also called "Soap."
WILD	Referring to a Joker which can be used in place of any tile (except in Jokerless hands).
WINDS	One category of Honors—the Norths, Easts, Wests and Souths.